Quit or Be Replaced

What Happens When Playing it

Safe Stops Working

by

BRIAN TURNER

For permissions, inquiries, or bulk orders, please contact:
hi@heybbt.com
www.heybbt.com

First Edition
ISBN: 979-8-9937162-3-7

Printed in the United States of America

Table of Contents

Introduction: The Day I Walked Away

I thought an MBA was the ticket.
All the stories in *Black Enterprise* told me so.
Men who looked like me in crisp button-downs, sitting on panels, building companies, and speaking the language of wealth. I bought that dream completely. I believed that hard work, education, and ambition would line up perfectly if I just played the game right.

After graduation, I was ready to step into a lucrative role, start climbing the corporate ladder, and make that magazine story my reality. But this was 2002, the Bush-era recession. Companies were cutting back, and jobs were scarce.

The plan was simple: climb the ladder, save, retire. But plans only work when the ground beneath them doesn't move.

My first opportunity came at **Fannie Mae.**
Deal Structuring Analyst.
Forty thousand dollars a year.

It was not the dream, but it was a start.
I told myself it was temporary. That I would prove myself, climb fast, and make the next leap in no time. Every night I stayed late. Every morning I showed up early. I learned the language of the

meetings, memorized the process, and smiled when it counted. It was the script we were all told to follow.

> "They said education was the key.
> No one told us the door would keep changing locks."

For a while, it worked. I was moving. Promoted to **Deal Structuring Manager** after a few years. The title looked better on paper, and I was surrounded by people who measured success by salary bands, cubicle size, and vacation time. But something about it never felt right.

Every year, the same recycled performance reviews:
"You're doing great work."
"Keep it up."
"Continue to develop in these areas."

It was like being stuck on a treadmill that led nowhere.
I realized the ladder I was climbing didn't have a top.

So I did what I thought I was supposed to do next.
I went higher.

I accepted a position at **OFHEO**, the **Office of Federal Housing Enterprise Oversight**, which regulated Fannie Mae and Freddie Mac. The irony wasn't lost on me. I went from working for the company to working for its regulator.

It was everything I thought I wanted.
A **$100,000** salary.
A corner office.
A clean title: **Senior Financial Risk Analyst**.
Respect. Stability. Power.

Everyone around me told me I had made it.
Especially in D.C., where a government job meant
lifetime security.

But I couldn't shake the feeling that something was
wrong. The energy was heavy. The hallways were
quiet. People just existed there. No spark, no
movement. Every conversation felt like it was
happening under fluorescent lights. The air in that
building felt filtered, clean but lifeless.

I promised myself I would stay one year.
Just long enough to stack some savings and
prepare for the next move.
No one believed me. People thought I was crazy for
even thinking about leaving.

During that year, I started reading everything I
could find about business and entrepreneurship. I
was trying to prepare for something I couldn't quite
define. I wanted to be free, but I didn't know what
freedom really cost.

In 2006, I made the decision to walk away.
No backup plan.
No guarantee.
Just conviction.

I told myself I would never work for anyone again.
And I meant it.

> "Freedom is never found in titles.
> It starts when you stop waiting for
> permission."

At the time, I thought I was chasing a dream.
Looking back, I was escaping a trap.

Because shortly after I left, everything fell apart.

In **September 2008**, the government placed **Fannie Mae** and **Freddie Mac** into conservatorship under the **Federal Housing Finance Agency**, which replaced OFHEO entirely. The financial system collapsed, and so did the illusion of safety.

Colleagues I used to eat lunch with lost their life savings.
Stock portfolios that were supposed to secure their retirement vanished overnight.
Friends who had mocked my decision to leave were suddenly without jobs, without purpose, and without a plan.

The entire system that had promised security revealed itself for what it was: temporary.

At first, I thought it was just bad luck, a one-time crash.
But now, almost twenty years later, I see it differently.

That moment was the preview of everything we are watching unfold right now.

I thought I'd seen the end of the old system. I was wrong.

Because the same collapse that took down housing is taking down jobs.
Except this time, it's not mortgage-backed securities.
It's automation.
It's AI.
It's algorithms replacing ambition.

> "Every decade brings a new kind of layoff. This time, it's digital."

In 2024 alone, more than **250,000 tech workers** were laid off.
Entire departments replaced by software that learns faster, costs less, and never calls in sick.
Consulting firms are downsizing teams. Marketing agencies are automating output. Even creative work like writing, design, video is being replicated by machines that don't sleep and don't need insurance.

It's happening again.
Different tools.
Same truth.

I recognized that pattern early. That quiet discomfort I felt in those offices wasn't rebellion; it was recognition. Somewhere deep down, I knew the structure was already rotting. The rules they told us to follow no longer applied.

And if I'm honest, most of us know it now too.

We can feel it in our meetings.
We can see it in our inboxes.
We can sense it when promotions vanish, roles get redefined, or your work gets absorbed by a new system with no face and no empathy.

The illusion of job security hasn't disappeared.
It's just evolved into a quieter kind of replacement.

I don't write this as someone who figured it all out.
I'm still building.
Still learning.
Still adapting.
But I know this much: what we call freedom isn't what they told us it was.

It's not working less.
It's working right.
It's building something that can't be automated.
It's finding peace in ownership, not performance.

When I left Fannie Mae, I didn't just quit a job.
I quit the belief that stability could be outsourced to someone else's system.

That was 2006.
And here we are again, another shift, another collapse, another generation of professionals

standing at the same crossroad, wondering if it's time to make their move.

This book is for them.

It's for the person staring at a computer screen, knowing their role is next.
It's for the quiet thinkers who feel out of place in meetings that no longer have meaning.
It's for the ones who followed the rules and still ended up anxious, uncertain, or replaceable.

You don't have to quit today.
You don't have to have it all figured out.
But you do have to build something that belongs to you.

Because what's coming, isn't a storm you can wait out.
It's a new economy that will reward those who are already preparing.

> "You will either quit or be replaced.
> The choice isn't between jobs.
> It's between control and comfort."

This book exists to help you build what can't be automated.
To show you what happens after the leap.
And to prove that the quiet decision to take back your time might be the loudest move you ever make.

Welcome to *Quit or Be Replaced.*
Let's begin.

Chapter 1: The Illusion of Job Security

The office was quiet in that particular way that only happens before bad news.
Phones still rang. The printer still hummed. But under it all, there was a stillness that felt heavier than usual.

It was a Thursday, the kind of day that starts ordinary and ends with a cardboard box.

He was in early, like always. Coffee mug in the same spot. Outlook open. A few unread messages, mostly routine. Then the subject line appeared in bold at the top of his screen:
Company Update: Organizational Changes.

He clicked it.
The email was short.
His department was being restructured. His position, along with dozens of others, was eliminated effective immediately.

No warning. No meeting. No handshake.
Just a link to schedule an HR call and a note about "support during this transition."

By noon, he was standing at his desk, slowly packing years of his life into a small box. Photos. A plaque from a company retreat. A coffee mug with his initials on it.

The same people who used to greet him at the elevator suddenly avoided eye contact.
No one was cruel. They were just scared.

He had played by every rule.
Showed up early. Stayed late.
Did the extra work without complaint.
He believed that would protect him.

That was the illusion.

For decades, we were told that hard work guaranteed stability.
That if you gave your best years to a company, that company would take care of you.
That loyalty mattered.

It sounded like a contract, but it never was one.

The truth is, job security was never real. It was just a rhythm, a pattern of steady paychecks that made you forget how fragile the system really was.

The phrase itself is misleading.
Security implies control, but in corporate life, control rarely belongs to the employee.
All it takes is one new CEO, one merger, or one spreadsheet full of red numbers, and the work you built your life around becomes a line item to be optimized.

It is not personal.
It is procedural.
And that is what makes it so dangerous.

> "They call it restructuring.
> But for the people inside it, it feels more
> like erasing."

Job security is not just a lie we were told. It is a story
we helped keep alive.
We passed it down like a survival strategy.
Work hard, stay quiet, be dependable, and
everything will work out.

That story worked when companies valued loyalty
because turnover was expensive and expertise was
rare.
But the world has changed.

The average person now holds twelve jobs in a
lifetime.
Entire industries shift overnight.
One announcement can erase ten years of
consistency.

In 2024 alone, hundreds of thousands of people in
banking, tech, and consulting found themselves on
the wrong side of an email like the one that man
opened on that Thursday morning.

Some of them were top performers.
Some had been there for decades.
None of it mattered.

What mattered was the spreadsheet.
The numbers won. They always do.

"The hardest truth about security is that
it only exists for the people who can take
it away."

The illusion works because it hides behind routine.
You convince yourself you are safe because you
have a title, a team, and a task list that resets every
Monday.
You mistake motion for meaning.

The meetings, the reports, the small promotions,
they create a rhythm that feels permanent.
You build your life around that rhythm.
A mortgage.
A car note.
Vacations on the same week every year.

Then one day, the rhythm stops.

And in that silence, you realize how much of your
identity was built around something that could
vanish in one email.

Job security is not just about money. It is about belonging.
When that belonging is taken away, it feels like more than unemployment. It feels like exile.

That is why people stay long after they know it is time to leave.
They are not staying for the paycheck.
They are staying for the illusion of being needed.

The system depends on that.
As long as you fear leaving more than you fear staying, you will keep the machine running.

There was a time when job security made sense.
When people retired with gold watches and farewell parties.
When companies carried a sense of family.

But that time is gone.

The modern workplace is not built for loyalty. It is built for efficiency.
And efficiency has no memory.

The same technology that made work faster also made people replaceable.
Not because they lack value, but because the system measures value differently now.

It measures it in time saved, costs reduced, and margins widened.
Human effort does not compete well in that equation.

> "What used to make you valuable now makes you vulnerable."

The illusion of job security is powerful because it feeds two of our deepest needs: safety and identity.
You want to believe that what you give your time to will give something back.
You want to believe that the years you invest in someone else's vision will eventually buy you freedom.

But that is not how it works anymore.

There is no straight path to retirement waiting at the end of forty years of good behavior.
There is no pension to protect you from inflation or automation.
Even the government jobs that once represented the safest bet have become unstable.

You can start rebuilding your sense of security around things that belong to you: your skills, your systems, your ideas, your ability to adapt.

That is not cynicism. It is reality.

The good news is, once you see the illusion for what it is, you can stop clinging to it.
You can start rebuilding your sense of security around things that belong to you — your skills, your systems, your ideas, your ability to adapt.

This is the moment when people either wake up or double down.
Some will fight to keep the illusion alive, hoping the next promotion or the next company will feel different.
Others will decide to build something real.

What separates the two is awareness.

You cannot change what you refuse to see.

And once you see it, you cannot unsee it.

The truth is, you were never hired for who you are.
You were hired for what you could produce.
As soon as the cost of your production outweighs the convenience of keeping you, the system moves on.

That realization hurts at first, but it also frees you.
Because once you stop chasing security in a place that cannot provide it, you can start building the kind that lasts.

The kind that can't be outsourced, automated, or optimized away.

This is not about quitting recklessly.
It is about seeing clearly.

Once you understand that the illusion was never designed to protect you, you can start to protect yourself differently.

You can start to build from ownership, not employment.
You can start to work from vision, not validation.
You can begin to replace false security with real stability.

That is where the rebuild begins.

"Security is not something you find.
It is something you create."

In the next chapter, we will talk about what is replacing traditional work, why it is happening faster than anyone expected, and how you can position yourself before the next shift arrives.

The illusion is breaking.
What you build next will determine whether you survive it or own it.

Chapter 2: The Replacement Economy

The meeting started like every other quarterly review.
A long conference table. Polite greetings. Coffee cups lined up beside identical laptops.

Someone dimmed the lights and a projector hummed to life.
Slide 1: Revenue.
Slide 2: Operating costs.
Slide 3: Headcount reduction: a quiet bullet point tucked between graphs and percentages.

No one flinched. The language was calm, and the phrases were polished.
Optimization. Streamlining. Efficiency gains.

On one side of the screen were three job titles.
On the other a single word: **Automation.**

A simple comparison chart showed how the company cut costs by replacing a team of analysts with a subscription to ChatGPT Enterprise and a few Zapier automations.

Someone took a slow sip of coffee, pretending to study the slide, as if focus could hide discomfort.
No one asked questions.
The savings were applauded.

Not one person in that room mentioned the names of the people behind those eliminated roles.

That is how replacement works now.
Not through confrontation, but through quiet math.

Efficiency Is the New Currency

Every generation of business worships something. For decades, it was growth. Then came culture. Now it's efficiency.

The new economy does not ask how many people you employ.
It asks how many tasks you can eliminate.

When companies realized that one person armed with the right tools could outperform a team of four, the math became too tempting to ignore.

Tools like **ChatGPT**, **Claude**, and **Jasper** can now draft reports, write content, analyze data, and summarize meetings in seconds.
Midjourney and **Runway** are designing marketing assets that once took agencies weeks.
Zapier, **Make**, and **Notion AI** quietly run the backend of operations that used to require whole departments.

The result is a new kind of productivity, one that rewards the efficient and erases the redundant.

Globally, analysts estimate that by 2030, up to **800 million jobs** could be displaced by automation. Entire sectors are already being rewritten by algorithms that never tire.

> "In this economy, the question is no longer, Who can do the job? It's, Who needs to?"

The Invisible Replacement

Replacement does not always announce itself. Sometimes it arrives as "role consolidation." Sometimes it looks like "budget realignment."

At **Amazon**, internal logistics teams were trimmed after AI scheduling systems reduced the need for human planners.
Goldman Sachs quietly cut hundreds of analyst roles as machine learning systems took over basic modeling.
UPS merged several dispatch positions once routing software had proved faster and more accurate.

On paper, these are business decisions.
In real life, they are identity crises.

Because every person behind those spreadsheets and dashboards thought their expertise made them safe.

The truth is, companies rarely replace people overnight.
They slowly build systems that make those people optional.

By the time the announcement arrives, the process has already been running for months.

The Human Cost of Efficiency

I see it from both sides now.
Running multiple businesses, I have learned to do more with less.

Where I once had full-time marketing staff, I now run campaigns using **ChatGPT**, **Canva**, and **Google Drive** templates I designed myself.
I used to rely on outside editors and graphic designers for content. Now I use **Leonardo AI** for visuals and **ElevenLabs** for voiceovers.
Even payroll, invoicing, and scheduling is mostly automated.

It sounds efficient, and it is.
But it also feels strange.

There are days when I look at my workflow and realize I am managing what used to be an entire team, from strategy to production to publishing, with fewer people than ever before.

Part of me is proud of that progress.
Another part of me misses the collaboration that once made the work feel human.

This is the trade-off of modern efficiency.
You gain speed, but you lose connection.
You save money but risk meaning.

> "Technology will not just replace your job.
> It will replace the feeling of being needed."

The New Winners

Not everyone is losing in this shift.
Some people are thriving because they stopped resisting it.

Freelancers who understand automation are scaling faster than agencies.
Creators who use AI tools are producing at studio-level quality from their bedrooms.
Consultants who blend human strategy with machine speed are delivering in hours what once took weeks.

These are not tech geniuses.
They are problem solvers who learned how to *think with* the tools instead of competing against them.

They build small, move fast, and pivot often.
They understand that ownership in this new world

means knowing how to combine creativity, systems, and adaptability.

This is the rise of what I call the **hybrid builder:** someone who uses technology to multiply impact without losing personal identity.

The hybrid builder is not afraid of replacement because they already replaced the parts of themselves that were slowing them down.

The Shift

Replacement is not just a corporate problem; it is cultural.
The same mindset that automates work is starting to automate life: relationships, attention, even self-expression.

We scroll instead of speak.
We copy instead of create.
We optimize everything until nothing feels personal.

The real danger is not being replaced by machines.
It is becoming machine-like ourselves.

That is why awareness matters.
You cannot fight what you refuse to acknowledge.

The replacement economy is here.
You can resist it, ignore it, or learn to use it.

The people who survive it will not be the smartest or the most connected.
They will be the ones who adapt the fastest.

> "Replacement is not coming for you.
> It is already here.
> The question is whether you will
> compete with it or create through it."

This is the turning point.
You now understand that the illusion of job security was never about safety.
It was about dependence.

The next step is to learn how to transition from being dependent on systems to designing your own.

In the next chapter, we will talk about what happens right after the realization: the hesitation, the denial, and the quiet fear that keep people from moving.

Because once you see the replacement economy clearly, the hardest part is admitting that you are part of it.

The age of replacement isn't coming.
It's already written in the code.

Chapter 3: The Denial Phase

The startup space smelled like ambition and burnout.
Cold brew on every desk. Headphones in. Hoodies up.

Rows of laptops glowed in that open-floor rhythm where everyone looked busy but no one looked certain. Someone was designing a pitch deck. Another was rewriting code for the fourth time. Everyone was chasing the same dream in different directions.

It was a Tuesday.
The founder had a call with investors scheduled for later that afternoon.

Revenue was down. Team morale was low. Slack messages went unanswered for hours. But if you asked him how things were going, he would still smile and say, "We're good. Just early."

That's what denial sounds like in 2025.

It is not loud.
It is quiet confidence built on fear.

He wasn't lying. He was protecting himself from the truth.

The Psychology of Delay

Denial doesn't always look like ignorance.
Sometimes it looks like discipline.
You can know exactly what needs to change and
still find a thousand reasons not to act.

You tell yourself the timing isn't right.
You convince yourself the next quarter will be
better.
You stay busy enough to feel productive without
ever addressing what's actually wrong.

For some, denial looks like staying in a job that
stopped growing long ago. You tell yourself the
benefits are good, the timing isn't right, the
economy is unstable. You wait for the next raise or
title that never changes what you feel.

It is the most dangerous phase of building because
it feels responsible.

> "You call it patience.
> Sometimes it is just fear dressed in logic."

The mind has a way of making stagnation look
strategic.
When the truth gets too heavy, you wrap it in words
like "planning," "positioning," and "preparation."

But deep down, you already know the answer.
You just haven't built enough courage to act on it.

This is why most people never truly rebuild.
They see the cracks but convince themselves they are cosmetic.

The Comfort Loop

Denial isn't lazy. It is loyal.
It keeps you attached to what used to work long after it has stopped working.

You stay because you've convinced yourself that consistency is a virtue.
You stay because starting over feels like failure.
You stay because you have convinced yourself that consistency is a virtue.

Every year, millions of professionals stay in positions that quietly replace them. Not all at once. Bit by bit, as their work becomes easier to automate or outsource.

It is the same pattern across every industry.
Employees stay in jobs they have outgrown.
Entrepreneurs hold onto businesses they no longer believe in.
Creators keep posting content they no longer enjoy.

Denial offers comfort because it gives you something familiar to fight for.
Even if that thing is already gone.

"The longer you defend what's dying, the harder it becomes to imagine what's next."

The comfort loop feeds on routine.
You wake up, check your messages, scroll through other people's progress, and promise yourself tomorrow will be different.
Then you repeat the same day.

It isn't failure; it's fear on autopilot.

When Denial Looks Like Discipline

For high performers, denial wears a suit of responsibility.
It sounds like strategy.
It looks like work.

You tell yourself you are being patient.
You tell yourself you are waiting for the right opportunity.
You tell yourself you are staying loyal.

But sometimes loyalty is just a slow way of avoiding change.

The truth is, people who care the most often get stuck the longest.
You believe your persistence will fix things that were never meant to last.

You keep optimizing a system that expired long ago.
You mistake exhaustion for effort.
You measure progress in hours instead of outcomes.

At some point, you stop building and start maintaining.

> "Maintenance feels safe because it looks like movement, but movement without direction is just noise."

The modern world rewards this kind of denial.
We praise consistency.
We celebrate discipline.
We post about perseverance.

But there is a difference between holding on and hanging in.
One builds strength. The other builds silence.

Personal Reflection: The Always Up Moment

I have been there too.

For years, I stayed in an industry that no longer aligned with who I was becoming.
Home care gave me everything, including experience, success, and stability, but eventually it started to take more than it gave.

I knew the season was ending, but I convinced myself to wait.
I told myself I needed a better exit plan.
I told myself I had a responsibility.
I told myself I was being wise.

In reality, I was scared to let go of what had worked.

On one episode of the *Always Up Podcast*, I talked about it openly.
The years of grinding, the weight of payroll, the quiet exhaustion that comes from managing people when your heart is no longer in the mission.
I realized I had stayed too long because I was addicted to the feeling of being needed.

When you build something from scratch, it becomes part of your identity.
Walking away from it feels like walking away from a part of yourself.

That episode was a turning point for me.
Saying it out loud made me see how much denial hides behind good intentions.

I wasn't lazy.
I wasn't lost.
I was loyal to an old version of me.

The Mirror

Denial isn't dramatic.
It doesn't announce itself with failure or collapse.
It arrives in small decisions that slowly create
distance between what you say you want and what
you actually do.

It's waking up tired but telling yourself you're fine.
It's holding onto a business, a job, or a habit that
quietly drains you.
It's knowing the next move and pretending you
need more time.
It's seeing the layoff headlines and still convincing
yourself your department is different. It is knowing
your passion left years ago but showing up anyway
because walking away feels like failure.

We all do it.
It is the brain's way of buying peace in the short
term.

But every delay costs something.
Momentum. Confidence. Clarity.

If you look closely, you will see where denial lives in
your own story.
It is the conversation you keep avoiding.
The project you say you'll start "next month."
The relationship or role you already know is over.

That is the mirror moment.
When you stop rationalizing and start recognizing.

> "Denial doesn't stop the change.
> It only delays your growth."

You cannot build something new until you admit what no longer fits.

And that honesty is what separates builders from survivors.

Because the longer you stay where you don't belong, the harder it becomes to believe you can belong anywhere else.

The denial phase always ends one of two ways.
You move by choice.
Or life moves you.

Sometimes that answer whispers what you already know: it's time to quit before you're replaced.

In the next chapter, we will talk about what happens when you finally accept the truth and decide to pivot: how to rebuild identity, structure, and momentum after you let go.

But for now, just look in the mirror.
See what you have been protecting.
Ask yourself who you are really waiting on.

The answer will tell you everything.

Chapter 4: The Pivot Mindset

The garage was a museum of old ambition.
Stacks of boxes lined the walls. A framed certificate sat crooked on a shelf. A dusty briefcase leaned against a chair that hadn't been used in years.

It wasn't just clutter. It was history.

Old work clothes from a career that no longer existed. Notebooks filled with ideas that never happened. A laptop that once held the future.

She stood in the middle of it all on a quiet Saturday morning, hands on her hips, staring at the space like it was someone else's life. She'd been meaning to clean it for months. But every time she walked in, she got distracted by the weight of it.

Not the dust. The meaning.

Every item reminded her of a version of herself she'd outgrown but never officially released.

That is what the pivot really looks like.
Not a grand decision. Not a headline moment.
Just a quiet reckoning with everything you said you wanted and no longer do.

The Mental Reset

Before you can pivot in life or business, you have to pivot in perspective.

The biggest obstacle isn't money, skill, or opportunity: it's attachment.
Attachment to the story you told yourself about who you are and what success should look like.

We get comfortable wearing identities like uniforms.
Employee. Manager. Founder. Expert.
Each one gives us validation, structure, and a sense of belonging.

But those same labels can trap you.

When the world shifts, your identity has to shift too.
If you try to carry the same mindset into a new season, it'll collapse under its own weight.

> "You can't pivot with your old identity still driving."

The pivot begins in the mind, not the market.
The first move isn't quitting your job or launching something new.
It's clearing mental space to think differently about what you actually want to build.

If you're stuck, start here: ask yourself which version of you is still showing up to do work that no longer fits.

Once you stop defending that version, you'll have energy again.

The Belief Reboot

The hardest part of a pivot isn't starting over.
It's redefining what "winning" means.

For years, success meant a title, a salary, or a list of achievements.
You built your identity around external confirmation.

But when everything shifts, those metrics stop mattering.

If you still measure success by someone else's scoreboard, every pivot will feel like failure.

You're not behind; you're just building something different.
And that requires a new rulebook.

Start with this question:
What do I actually want my days to look like?

Not the highlight reel. The day-to-day.

If your answer doesn't match the life you're living, that's your cue.

> "The pivot isn't about leaving everything behind.
> It's about taking yourself back."

She didn't know it yet, but cleaning that garage was her first small act of resignation, a mental letting go before she ever drafted the letter.

The Small Pivot First Principle

Most people fail not because they refuse to pivot but because they try to do it all at once.

They quit the job, sell the business, and go all-in before they've built the muscle for change.
Then they panic, retreat, and call it a bad idea.

Real pivots happen in stages.

Start small.
Adjust one thing at a time.
Build momentum quietly.

If you're still working a nine-to-five, start your rebuild before you resign.
If you own a business, create one new stream of income before you shut the old one down.
If you're creative, release one piece of work on your terms before chasing a new brand.

Small pivots compound.
Each one builds confidence.
Each one teaches you how to move with less fear.

> "Don't burn the bridge.
> Just start walking across it."

The pivot mindset is about patience in motion: steady shifts that create stability instead of chaos.

The Strategic Pivot

Once you've accepted the need to move, the next step is clarity.

You can't build what you haven't defined.

Start by writing down three lists:

1. What stays

2. What goes

3. What grows

What stays represents the skills, relationships, and systems that still serve you.
What goes are the roles, obligations, and habits that drain you.
What grows are the opportunities that align with who you are becoming.

If you struggle to separate them, ask this question: Would I choose this again today if I were starting over?

If the answer is no, let it go.

The pivot is not about control. It's about clarity.
Once you know what truly matters, you can stop
wasting time trying to fix what was never meant to
be saved.

For some, that means staying.
For others, it means sending the email, packing the
desk, and walking out lighter.

> "Don't run from something.
> Move toward something."

That one mindset shift changes everything.

The Courage Rebuild

Every pivot comes with fear.
That fear isn't a signal to stop; it's proof that you're
alive and in motion.

The people who never pivot are not fearless. They
are numb.
They have learned how to silence the part of
themselves that wants more.

You cannot avoid fear, but you can reassign it.
Let fear remind you that you are moving in new
territory.
Let it sharpen you instead of stopping you.

The first few steps will always feel shaky.
That's how you know they matter.

"If the next step doesn't scare you a little, it's probably not a pivot. It's a pause."

The Pivot Framework: Three Questions Before You Pivot

Before you make any major move, sit with these three questions.
Write your answers. Read them twice. Then decide.

1. **What am I pretending still works?**
   Be brutally honest. The things you defend the most are often the ones holding you back.

2. **What am I afraid to lose that I've already outgrown?**
   Fear disguises itself as logic. But most of what you're afraid to lose has already stopped serving you.

3. **What could I build if I stopped trying to fix what's broken?**
   This is the real pivot. The shift from maintenance to creation.

If you can answer those questions truthfully, you'll know what to do next.

The pivot mindset isn't about quitting; it's about reclaiming direction before someone else defines it for you.

And sometimes, reclaiming direction means being brave enough to quit before you're quietly replaced.

In the next chapter, we'll talk about how to translate this new mindset into real movement: how to build small, move fast, and create momentum before fear catches up.

For now, just remember:
The pivot is not punishment.
It's permission.

Chapter 5: Build Small, Move Fast

The apartment was quiet except for the low hum of a laptop fan.
It was 11:47 p.m.

Everyone else was asleep, but she was still at the kitchen table, eyes tired, fingers typing.
A single lamp cast a soft circle of light across her notes.
Beside her, an empty mug of coffee and a page of sketches with names, links, numbers, and half-formed ideas.

She wasn't chasing a dream.
She was building an escape plan.

The kind you can't post about yet.
The kind you create in silence while everyone else thinks you're fine.

This is how most real stories begin: not with investors, not with launch parties, but with one person staying up late to figure it out.

She didn't need perfect.
She needed proof.

The Myth of the Big Launch

Most people never build anything because they're waiting for the big moment.
The announcement. The logo. The perfect website.

They tell themselves they'll start when things calm down, when they've saved more, when they finally "have time."
But time never appears.
Only choices do.

The truth is, the big launch is an illusion.
The internet makes it look like everything happens overnight, but every success you see started as something small, uncertain, and unpolished.

You don't need to launch big; you need to start small.

> "Clarity comes from creation, not contemplation."

The first version of anything you build is supposed to be rough.
The point isn't to impress anyone.
It's to see what works while the stakes are low.

Every side business, digital product, or freelance project you admire began as a test that someone was brave enough to run.

Build in the Quiet

Your best work will happen before anyone knows about it.
That's where the real foundation gets built, in silence, without applause, without pressure.

Start by asking yourself:
What can I create in the next seven days that helps someone solve a problem I understand?

Don't think in years; think in hours.

You don't need a company; you need a concept.
You don't need a team; you need a tool.

If you're working a job, your quiet hours are your building hours.
That's where the pivot becomes real.

Try this:

- Create one **affiliate link** and share it in your content this week.

- Build one **simple landing page** using free AI tools.

- Offer one **digital service** based on something you already know.

Small wins are how you gather proof that your ideas work.

The moment you earn your first sale, commission, or thank-you message from something you built, your brain starts to change.

You stop thinking like an employee.
You start thinking like a builder.

Speed as Strategy

Speed isn't about rushing.
It's about refusing to let fear catch up.

You don't need to move fast because you're behind; you move fast so you can learn quickly, fail smaller, and adjust in real time.

Waiting for perfection is how people end up staying in jobs they hate for ten extra years.

She learned that the hard way.
Every time she hesitated, another quarter slipped by.
Every time she told herself she wasn't ready, someone else was already building.

Speed reveals truth.
The faster you act, the faster you'll see if an idea deserves your energy.

> "You can fix almost anything except hesitation."

If you're trying to figure out what to build, stop thinking and start testing.

Launch one small offer. Send one email. Post one idea.

You'll know within days what people respond to.

The goal is not perfection.

It's momentum.

The $100 Test

You can test almost any idea for less than $100.

Pick one problem people keep asking you about. Use AI tools to create something that helps solve it. A guide. A checklist. A short video.

Here's the process:

1. **Validate** — Ask five people if they'd pay for the result your idea promises.

2. **Build** — Use Canva, Notion, or ChatGPT to design a simple version.

3. **Post** — Share it quietly with a small audience or on one social platform.

4. **Track** — If even one person pays or signs up, you've proven value.

That's all it takes to start separating imagination from proof.

This isn't about making millions.
It's about earning confidence.

> "The first dollar you make on your own changes everything."

You'll realize freedom isn't as far away as you thought; it's just buried under delay.

Momentum Rules

Momentum isn't speed; it's consistency over time.

Once you start building, make it part of your daily rhythm:

- **Show up** even when no one's watching.

- **Document** your progress privately.

- **Simplify** before you scale.

- **Automate** anything that slows you down.

Most people overestimate what they can do in a week and underestimate what they can accomplish in six months.

If you focus on small, consistent movement, the results will compound faster than you expect.

Momentum creates belief.
Belief creates courage.
Courage makes quitting the obvious next step.

Momentum will make the decision clear.
You won't have to guess when to quit.
You'll feel the pull toward something that finally is yours.

By the time you finally resign, you won't be walking away empty.
You'll be walking toward something you already proved.

The 7-Day Builder Challenge

If you want to start moving now, try this:

Day 1: Write down one skill or idea people ask you for help with.
Day 2: Create one simple solution using free tools or templates.
Day 3: Share it privately with five people and ask for feedback.
Day 4: Improve it based on what they say.
Day 5: Put a price on it, even $10 counts.
Day 6: Post it publicly or send it to one group.
Day 7: Reflect on what worked and what didn't.

If you finish all seven days, you'll have something real, something you built while everyone else was still planning.

And if you can do it once, you can do it again.

> "The fastest way to replace your job is to stop thinking it's the only place your value lives."

In the next chapter, we'll talk about what happens after you start building. We'll talk about how to design a life around the work you create, not the work you escape.

Because freedom isn't found in quitting; it's found in building small, moving fast, and never slowing down once you start.

Chapter 6: Design Your Freedom

The first morning felt quiet in a way he hadn't felt in years.
No alarm. No commute. No calendar full of other people's priorities.

He made coffee slowly, not because he wanted to waste time but because he finally had it.
The air felt different. Lighter. Still.

This was what freedom looked like.
At least, what he thought it would.

But as the silence stretched, something unexpected appeared.
A question.

Now what?

He realized quitting was never the finish line.
It was the starting point for something new, and something fragile.

Freedom without direction can feel like being lost.

The Myth of Freedom

Most people think freedom means doing whatever you want, whenever you want.
But that version fades fast.

Real freedom isn't about escape; it's about design.

If you quit your job only to wake up without structure, you'll drift right back into old habits: distraction, doubt, and overthinking.

He learned that the hard way.
For months after leaving his last job, he celebrated being free from the meetings and the deadlines.
But without a rhythm, days started to blur.
Work piled up, and focus disappeared.

That's when he realized something simple but powerful:
Freedom without discipline feels like chaos.
Discipline without freedom feels like a job.

The goal is to design a life that balances both.

> "Freedom is not the absence of work.
> It's the presence of purpose."

Build a Rhythm, Not a Routine

You can't live free if your days still control you.

The secret isn't to plan every hour; it's to design your energy around what matters most.

He started using a system he called *Builder Time Blocks*.
Each day, he focused on three simple categories:

1. **Income** — one task that moves money.

2. **Improvement** — one task that builds a new skill or system.

3. **Inspiration** — one task that keeps the mind alive.

That was it, three wins a day.

Some days the income task meant finishing a client project.
Some days it meant sending a single offer.
But every day had structure, just enough to feel focused, not boxed in.

This rhythm built momentum again, the same kind he used to build when working late nights during his transition.
Only now, the energy went toward something he owned.

> "When you stop living by other people's calendars, you start hearing your own ideas again."

Money That Moves With You

The biggest trap after quitting is recreating the same stress with a new logo.

If your new freedom still depends on trading hours for dollars, you're just wearing a different badge.

He learned to build income that moved with him — small systems that kept working when he didn't.

At first, that meant writing digital guides, building affiliate links, and creating small offers.
Then it became about automation, using AI tools, templates, and workflows that multiplied effort without needing more hours.

It wasn't fast, but it was real.
And real freedom isn't measured in followers or paychecks.
It's measured in control.

When your money can move without you, you start thinking differently.
You stop chasing security and start building systems that create it.

> "The goal isn't to make more money.
> It's to make money mean less."

Protecting Your Energy

Freedom comes with new temptations to overwork, to overshare, to say yes to everything that feels like opportunity.

But if you're not careful, you'll build another cage with your own hands.

He used to think burnout came from bad jobs.
Now he knows it comes from broken boundaries.

Every yes carries a cost.
Every new project requires a piece of you.

Protecting your energy is part of protecting your business.
Delegate when you can; automate what you must.
And don't confuse movement with meaning.

You left your job to regain peace.
Don't lose it trying to prove you made the right decision.

The Freedom Framework

Freedom doesn't organize itself.
You have to design it.

Here's a simple system to maintain balance while you build.

1. The Builder's Morning:
Start the day by defining your three priorities:

- One for income

- One for improvement

- One for inspiration

Don't touch notifications or social feeds until all three are clear.

2. The Power Hour:
Spend sixty minutes on deep work that actually moves results.
No distractions. No multitasking. Just focus.

3. The Exit Check:
End each day with a single question:
Did I build something that will still matter tomorrow?

If the answer is yes, you're designing freedom, not drifting through it.

> "You don't build freedom once.
> You practice it daily."

The Quiet Realization

He finished his coffee and walked to the window.
The sun was high now.
No one was waiting on him.

The silence that once felt heavy now felt earned.

He wasn't chasing a promotion or a title anymore.
He was building something that finally felt like his.

This was the test all along.
To see if he could build a life that worked without permission.

Freedom was never the goal.
It was the test, to see what you'd do when no one was watching.

Chapter 7: The Rebuild Blueprint

The room was smaller than his last office, but it felt bigger.
No framed awards, no company mission on the wall.
Just a desk, a laptop, a whiteboard, and a window that let in the morning light.

He was back at square one.
Only this time, the square was his.

Across the city, she sat at her own kitchen table.
A notebook open. A candle lit.
Her rebuild was quieter, but just as intentional.

Two different rooms.
Same beginning.

The Identity Rebuild

When you leave the system, you lose more than a paycheck.
You lose a piece of who you thought you were.

The titles go first.
Then the schedule.
Then the certainty.

For a while, that emptiness feels heavy.
You question if you made the right decision.
You wonder if you should have stayed just a little longer.

But that space is sacred.
It is where you rebuild who you are without the noise of validation.

He stopped introducing himself by job title.
He started describing what he built, whom he helped, and what he was learning.
That small shift changed everything.

She rebuilt differently.
She stopped apologizing for not fitting into corporate boxes.
She began writing her own job description, one that actually matched her values.

> "When your worth no longer depends on your role, freedom finally begins."

Identity is not a brand. It is a blueprint.
And the first part of rebuilding is remembering who you were before the job told you who to be.

The Financial Rebuild

Quitting teaches you more about money than any job ever could.

Every dollar matters differently when you earn it yourself.

At first, the focus was survival.
Then it became stability.
Eventually, it turned into strategy.

He created what he called **The Three-Stream Rule**:

- One **consistent** stream that paid the bills.

- One **creative** stream that made him grow.

- One **automated** stream that worked while he rested.

It kept things simple.
No chasing twenty side hustles.
No comparison with others who seemed to be further ahead.

She took a different path.
Her rebuild was slower but sharper.
She learned to detach emotion from income and focus on alignment.
Some months were light; others overflowed.
But she always felt rich in clarity.

> "You do not need more income streams.
> You need better systems for the ones you have."

If the job once gave you security, the rebuild gives you control.
And control is the real currency of freedom.

The System Rebuild

Structure wasn't the enemy.
It was the missing piece.

He learned that freedom without systems turns into chaos fast.
Emails pile up. Ideas scatter. Energy fades.

So he built light systems that protected his focus.

- A weekly review every Sunday resets goals.

- A single spreadsheet to track income and expenses.

- Automations for tasks that drained attention.

- A rule that nothing new entered the week unless it replaced something old.

The systems were not fancy.
They were sustainable.

She didn't love structure at first.
Her creativity resisted it.
But when she saw how her ideas got lost without

process, she built her own flow, playlists, morning pages, small rituals that gave her chaos rhythm.

He built spreadsheets.
She built space instead.
Both found freedom.

> "Systems do not limit freedom.
> They keep it from falling apart."

The Mindset Rebuild

No one talks enough about the loneliness that follows quitting.
There is no team chat, no office energy, no one to tell you, "Good job."

At first, the silence feels like peace.
Then it starts to feel like pressure.

He had to rebuild his mind as much as his work.
He learned to replace noise with intention.
He learned to celebrate small wins.
He learned that slow progress is still progress.

She faced the same silence but filled it differently.
She journaled through doubt.
She made peace with the pace.
She learned that not every day needed to prove something.

There were days when doubt whispered louder than ambition.
But those were the days that mattered most.
Because rebuilding isn't about speed.
It is about endurance.

> "Discipline is how you prove to yourself
> that freedom was worth it."

The Rebuild Blueprint

Use this as a framework for the next chapter of your life.
Write it down. Sit with it. Live it.

Identity
Ask yourself: *Who am I becoming without the job?*
The answer will evolve, but it must start from truth.
You are not your title, your pay grade, or your position. You are what remains when the system fades.

Money
Ask yourself: *What three streams can sustain me long term?*
One steady. One creative. One automated. Keep it lean. Simplicity is sustainability.

System
Ask yourself: *What can I simplify, automate, or delegate?*

You are the engine now. Protect your time. Build rhythm before you build scale.

Mindset
Ask yourself: *What daily habits keep me clear and grounded?*
These are your anchors. Small routines will keep you steady when uncertainty shows up again.

Purpose
Ask yourself: *Who or what benefits from what I build?*
If the answer is only you, rebuild again. The work should ripple.

When you finish, you'll have more than answers.
You'll have direction.
Because freedom is not one big leap.
It is a series of small rebuilds done right.

The Quiet Realization

He looked around the room again.
Nothing about it was impressive, yet everything about it was intentional.

This time there were no meetings waiting, no titles to chase, no illusion of safety to protect.
Only space to think.
And structure to grow.

She did the same across the city.
No noise. No validation.
Just music playing low and a list of ideas for tomorrow.
Her rebuild had taken longer, but it finally felt steady.

Both smiled.
Because this was not a comeback.
It was construction.

> "You can lose the job, the title, or even the plan.
> But if you rebuild with alignment, you'll never lose yourself again.."

Chapter 8: The Future of Work

The building was still there.
But the people were not.

Rows of desks sat perfectly clean.
The hum of conversation had been replaced by the sound of machines, quiet, constant, and tireless.
Monitors flickered with dashboards that once required teams.
Reports that took weeks now updated in seconds.

What used to be work became data.
And what used to be workers had become history.

The Great Replacement

Over the last decade, technology didn't just speed up work. It absorbed it.

Artificial intelligence now writes code, answers calls, analyzes spreadsheets, creates ads, edits videos, and even conducts interviews.
Entire departments that once took hundreds of people can now run on five.

In 2024 alone, more than **250,000 tech workers were laid off**, with most of those roles replaced not by new hires but by new tools.

Across industries, **nearly 40 percent of tasks** are already automated or handled by algorithms.

We were told automation would make life easier, but no one explained it would also make people optional.

The new threat isn't losing your job.
It's being quietly replaced by a process that never calls in sick, never questions policy, and never asks for more pay.

That's not science fiction.
That's payroll reality.

> "AI doesn't steal jobs. It absorbs patterns.
> The more predictable you are, the faster you disappear."

The New Hierarchy of Work

Every generation creates its own class system.
Ours is no longer built on money or on education.
It's built on creation.

The economy is reorganizing into three layers:

Creators — the ones who invent, build, and design new systems.
Connectors — the ones who translate those systems for others.

Consumers — the ones who depend on what is built without ever owning the means to build.

Most people were taught to consume.
Some were trained to connect.
Very few were raised to create.

But that's where the future lives: in creation, not compliance.

This is why quitting isn't rebellion anymore.
It's evolution.
The ones who leave first become the ones who lead later.

> "The new job security is not employment.
> It's ownership."

The Rise of Synthetic Success

Somewhere along the way, the world confused activity with achievement.

We scroll through highlights that look like hustle, but most of what we see is automation.
Posts written by AI. Metrics inflated by bots. Courses built on recycled content.

Synthetic success happens when imitation outpaces intention.

Quiet quitting was never about laziness.
It was about recognition.

People realized they were performing for a system that stopped clapping back.

Now the pendulum is swinging.
The ones who choose quiet creation over quiet quitting are shaping what comes next.

The future belongs to the builders, not the performers.

What Will Never Be Replaced

For all its power, AI still lacks what makes us human.
It cannot feel conviction.
It cannot imagine new meaning.
It cannot build belief.

It can replicate intelligence, but not intent.

The world will always need people who can see patterns, connect emotions, and translate chaos into clarity.
It will always need storytellers, strategists, creators, and those who lead with empathy.

Technology will take over repetition.
But humanity will always own resonance.

If you can think for yourself, build from truth, and create with care, you're already rare.

> "The future will automate everything
> except authenticity."

The Builder's Edge

The builders are not the ones shouting online.
They are the ones learning in silence, testing ideas,
and stacking small wins.

They move fast, but not recklessly.
They create systems, not just content.
They build brands that feel like belief, not
performance.

They do not compete with machines because they
do not think like them.
Their advantage is awareness.

AI can write, but it cannot *want*.
It can learn, but it cannot *long*.

And that difference, the space between intention
and imitation, will define the next decade.

Builders who master this balance will not just
survive the future; they will design it.

The Vision Ahead

We are living through the most significant shift in
work since the Industrial Revolution.
Except this time, the machines are not in factories.
They are in our pockets, our browsers, and our daily
habits.

You can choose to compete with them or collaborate through them.
You can resist the change or ride the wave of it.
But you cannot ignore it.

This is not the age of employees.
It is the age of builders, independent, adaptable, creative thinkers who build structures that cannot be replaced by code.

To quit is not to give up.
It is to graduate.
It is to step out of the assembly line and into authorship.

> "The future will not reward the loyal.
> It will reward the aligned."

And if you've made it this far, you already understand the truth.
You were never meant to stay; you were meant to build.

So build something that lasts.
Build something that matters.
Build something that no algorithm can replicate.

Because the future will not wait for permission.
But it will always make room for those who build.

The Exit Plan (Before You Leap)

The email sat in the draft folder for three days.
The subject line was simple: "Resignation."
No long explanation. No emotion. Just a date.

He read it over and over, waiting for peace to arrive.
It never did.

The truth is, peace never comes before you leap.
It only meets you once you move.

That is why quitting is not a single decision.
It is slow preparation of the mind, the money, and the mission.

You have come this far for a reason.
You have seen the cracks. You have felt the quiet ache of staying somewhere that no longer fits.
You have started to imagine what life could look like on your own terms.

But quitting is not an act of impulse.
It is an act of preparation.

You do not leave because you are tired.
You leave because you are ready.

And readiness is built long before the resignation letter.

---

1. Know Your Number

Freedom has a cost.
Not emotional, but practical.

Write down what you truly need to live for six months: rent, food, gas, insurance, utilities, debt, and peace.
Add it up. That is your freedom figure.

When you see it clearly, it stops being a fantasy and becomes a number you can build toward.
Numbers turn fear into focus.

Clarity doesn't kill faith; it strengthens it.

---

2. Build the Bridge

Do not hate the job that funds your freedom.
Use it.

Every paycheck is a brick in the bridge from dependence to direction.
Redirect a small portion of what you earn into what you are building: the website, the gear, the knowledge, the savings.

You are not working for the company anymore.
You are working through it.

Every hour on the clock can be an investment if you treat it like one.
A quiet builder uses the system until they no longer need it, then leaves without bitterness.

That is how you turn a job into a stepping stone instead of a cage.

---

3. Protect the Runway

Courage without a cushion turns into panic.
Give yourself time to breathe.

Three to six months of expenses are the difference between creativity and desperation.
You do not have to reach perfection, only preparation.

When you know you can survive, you move differently.
You stop making emotional decisions.
You start creating from a place of calm.

Money doesn't buy peace, but margin does.
Build your margin before you build your escape.

---

4. Leave with Grace

The best exits are quiet.
No speeches, no posts, no dramatic exits.

Thank the people who mattered.
Close the loops.
Walk away without noise.

The world is smaller than it looks.
The same person who doubts you today might
recommend you tomorrow.

Leaving well is not weakness. It is wisdom.
You are not leaving to prove a point.
You are leaving to start a new chapter.

---

5. The First Thirty Days

After you quit, the silence will feel strange.
You'll wake up earlier than you expect.
You will check your phone for meetings that no
longer exist.
You will feel invisible for a while.

That is not failure. It is withdrawal.
You are detoxing from dependency.

Use the first month to build rhythm.
Set your own hours.
Create structure before success.
Track the small things: what you learned, what you
earned, what you finished.

Small wins rebuild confidence.
Confidence rebuilds identity, and identity keeps you
moving when motivation fades.

The Reminder

You do not quit a job to run from work.
You quit to redefine it.

You quit because the system was never designed for builders.
It was designed for safety.
And safety is not the same as purpose.

So count your cash.
Cut your noise.
Commit your plan.

Then leap like someone who already tested the landing.

> "Freedom is not in leaving; it is in being ready when you do."

This short chapter is only the beginning.
In the *Built from Scratch* series, I will be writing a full companion book, a step-by-step guide that breaks down exactly how to quit your job with structure, strategy, and peace of mind.

If *Quit or Be Replaced* gave you the mindset, that one will give you the method.

Final Reflection: The Builder's Manifesto

Freedom was never the goal.
It was the test.

Could you walk away from what felt safe and still trust what you could not yet see?
Could you rebuild from belief instead of approval?
Could you keep going when the noise stopped and no one was watching?

That's what this journey was always about.
Not quitting.
Becoming.

I didn't know it when I left that first job in 2006 and decided I would never take another paycheck again.
I thought I was leaving for money, for meaning, for control.
But what I was really doing was learning how to stand on my own convictions.
I was learning how to build peace the same way I once built productivity.

And peace costs more than any paycheck ever did.

The world told me freedom meant ease.
It doesn't.
It means responsibility.
It means carrying the weight of your choices and the faith that they will eventually matter.

It means learning that you don't need permission to move.

If you've made it this far, you've already proven something most people never do: that comfort is not enough.
That you were willing to trade certainty for purpose.
That you were ready to rebuild even when you didn't have a map.

That's what makes you a builder.
You don't wait for direction.
You create it.

The builders are the ones who choose alignment over applause.
They do the work that others avoid.
They learn, they fall, they adapt, and they rise again.
They understand that no system can define their worth.

So if you are somewhere in between quitting and becoming, if you are rebuilding in silence, if you are figuring out what to do with the freedom you asked for...keep going.
Silence is not punishment.
It's preparation.

Every skill, every failure, every quiet day is a brick in the next version of you.
And when it starts to take shape, when you start to see the structure of who you are becoming, you will

understand that this was never about leaving something behind.

It was about building something that lasts.

Something that works without permission.
Something that cannot be replaced.
Something that carries your name long after the system forgets you.

"You're not quitting. You're reclaiming."

This is your blueprint.
This is your test.
This is your time.

Acknowledgments

To everyone who ever told me to play it safe, thank you.
You gave me something worth proving wrong.

To the builders who read this and saw a piece of their own story, I wrote this for you.
For the ones still showing up after the noise fades.
For the ones who rebuild when no one is clapping.
For the ones who keep betting again.

To every coworker, friend, and mentor who crossed my path, thank you for shaping the lessons that became this book.

To my children, Bryce and Bria, everything I build, I build with you in mind.
I want you to know that freedom is possible, but it must be protected.
You're my reason to keep getting up and trying again.

To my family, near and far, who believed even when they did not always understand, I love you for that.

To God, the quiet foundation beneath every fall and rebuild, thank you for peace in the middle of the noise.

Notes

Quit or Be Replaced was written during one of the most uncertain and defining seasons of my life. It's not advice; it's experience rebuilt into clarity.

If this book spoke to you, share it with another builder.
You never know who is one quiet decision away from freedom.

For speaking, media, or collaborations, visit **heybbt.com**.

For more books, digital products, or apparel, explore the **Built from Scratch** series and **BBT APPAREL**.

Stay connected, stay building, stay aligned.

Always up.

www.ingramcontent.com/pod-product-compliance
Lightning Source LLC
Chambersburg PA
CBHW071609200326
41519CB00021BB/6928